21 Lessons
To Empower
The New Age Kid

21 Lessons
To Empower
The New Age Kid

Sandra K. Jones-Keller

For information about this book or other services, contact the author at SandraJonesKeller.com.

21 Lessons To Empower The New Age Kid

Cover Design: Thomas Keller
Facebook—Thomas Keller Artist

ISBN: 1541020502
ISBN 9781541020504

ALSO BY SANDRA K. JONES-KELLER

Intuitive Communication With Your Baby's Soul

Dedication

*The New Age is upon us and I dedicate this
book to all the children answering the call, especially
my daughter, Mecca, who inspires me each and every day.*

Contents

Acknowledgements

I love that I hadn't planned on writing this book. I wish to thank Patti Cohen for inviting me to facilitate weekly presentations for her homeschool cooperative that I then used to create this program of 21 lessons. And thank you to all the kids and parents that participated with me.

A special thanks to my daughter, Mecca, for working with me to create the lessons for the original presentations, and for just being awesome!

Loving thanks to Thomas Keller for being my supportive husband and a kick-ass artist. He turned my chicken scratches into a beautiful piece of art for the cover design.

Much love to my Wednesday night writer's group led by the inimitable Kristine Gill. Thanks for letting me read my non-fiction workbook in your fiction group.

I am grateful to Evelyn Thompson-Hilbert and Amy Anstead for your invaluable feedback and notes, and thank you to Alison Blanco for being my friend and editor.

Introduction

The last couple of decades have brought in new energies of creativity, enlightenment, and connectedness with our higher selves. Many of the children being born are more advanced and aware than any generation before them. They are demanding new paradigms in education and business that support who they are as spiritual beings and their life purpose. Anything else will be met with resistance or refusal to participate.

Although any child would benefit from learning the life principles discussed in this book, it is targeted to the New Age kid. I wanted to address children like my daughter: old souls that are wise beyond their years, are connected with and aware of their divine essence, have a remembrance of past lives, are clear, certain, intuitive, kind, forgiving, gentle, loving, and naturally joy-filled and generous. Some even demonstrate psychic and healing abilities at a very early age.

New Age children are everywhere! They're in public schools and private schools, youth groups and church groups, sports clubs and academic clubs. Many are homeschooled because they just don't fit into societal norms or because their parents want something different for them.

These kids have been incarnating for many, many years and have been called different names: Indigo Children, Crystal Children, Star Children and Rainbow Children. Each generation has attributes that are different from the previous one, but they have all come here to assist with the ascension of our planet!

—⟋⟋—

PROGRAM OBJECTIVES AND IMPACT OF THE 21 LESSONS PRESENTED IN THIS BOOK:

- This program of life principles is designed to supersede all personal stories and bring out a child's enlightened self.
- These heart-centered conversations activate soul remembrance and tap into the quantum field (multi-dimensionality) in which everything is available.
- Children will get to experience how powerful and valuable they truly are, not because of anything they've accomplished, but because that is the nature of their being.
- The topics and discussions assist a child to get out of blame and step into a creative space of living a purposeful life, thereby being a contribution to humanity.

—⟋⟋—

HOW DO THESE SHORT LESSONS CREATE CHANGE IN A CHILD'S LIFE?

Because we live in a mental Universe, everything around us was once a thought: the chairs we sit in, the clothes we wear, our computers, the internet, old and new inventions. Everything in our lives is a reflection of our thoughts, beliefs and vibration (emotional state) being mirrored back to us.

When a child (or anyone) makes a conscious choice to change their thoughts and beliefs from negative to positive and/or supportive, they begin to raise their vibration. Their world starts to change. The potentials of one path shift as their consciousness (awareness and awakeness) shifts. As this happens, the child is no longer doomed to repeat past cycles of disappointment, sadness or upset. They can break out of old family patterns and create new levels of health and well-being, peace, joy and prosperity. Everyone and everything benefits from this personal healing and awakening!

A Personal Note to Parents and Group Facilitators

The raw material for this program of 21 Lessons To Empower The New Age Kid was taken from a series of weekly presentations given to my daughter's homeschool group with an age range of four to seventeen years old. I was originally asked to facilitate meditations for the kids, but ended up calling them mindfulness exercises to cover a broader range. My challenge was keeping the presentations short and effective to keep the kids engaged. Additionally, with this group I had to consider my language so as not to alienate participants (kids and some parents). The families ranged from those who were secular, non-spiritual, to those of different observant religious backgrounds and everything in between.

You'll notice I have taken more liberty with the language I use in the written version of these lessons. Concepts that I talk about in my inner circle like mirroring, divine self, intuition, quantum field, chakra and multi-dimensional are now sprinkled throughout. However, you as the parent or facilitator can use language and terms that you deem appropriate for your particular child or group of kids. This will not impact the veracity or effectiveness of the lessons. Let's say you don't like the term divine self. If you substitute divine for authentic (self) or true (self), then the concept remains the same while still conveying the overall message.

For the first few weeks of the presentations I came up with the topics. Then I asked my daughter what she wanted to talk about. I was surprised by the topics she came up with, they weren't on my radar at all: subjects like anger, boredom, friendship and downtime. I had a blast creating the lessons with her—picking her 10-year-old brain and gaining insights into how she thinks and processes information. This book is arranged in the original order in which the exercises were presented.

At first, I felt the kids weren't understanding or just weren't interested until I heard one girl telling her friend to ground herself, and the program facilitator shared how her nephew had mentioned a couple of the concepts. Parents began thanking me for the weekly life principles discussed with their kids.

My husband described the presentations as giving the kids language for what they already feel and know intuitively. I agree with him totally!

Overview

Each of the 21 Lessons is divided into three parts: a discussion, an exercise and a work-sheet. The discussion introduces the topic with a question. Several questions follow so that you can engage your kids in a conversation. Next, you have a short exercise to practice the lesson, and lastly a worksheet to follow up on the exercise, which includes suggestions to use outside of class. I recommend that you copy and hand out the worksheets so that the kids can take them home to review and anchor in the principles.

The lessons can be done in 21 days or 21 weeks depending on your child's desired pace or the type of group you lead and how often it meets.

The intention of this program is to tap into the Universal Intelligence of each child. Don't worry about trying to make your conversations perfect or think you have to have all the answers. You are creating a partnership with your child or group toward their personal development and enlightenment. You, as the parent or facilitator, are not solely responsible for the depth of the conversation. The more the children contribute, the bigger the leaps to their own self-realization.

For some kids, this may be the first time they are held accountable for their involvement level—for the outcome of their experience. Too often kids sit around thinking it's the adults' responsibility to make things fun or interesting for them.

This is certainly not the case with this program. As the child opens up and shares from their heart, leaning in and adding to the conversation, they will receive the direct benefits. It is their opportunity to be responsible for what they learn and grasp.

How to Use This Workbook

- This is a fluid program—look at it as a road map to empowering conversations as opposed to a traditional workbook. Leave room for spontaneous topics. If there's a current event pressing in the news, consider how to weave that into an empowering conversation with your child or group. Additionally, weave previous topics into current discussions. Make connections and relationships among the topics to help anchor them in.
- **Plan on keeping your lessons short, 15-20 minutes including the exercise and worksheet.** Since the dynamics of each group will be different play around to find the best fit for your kids.
- Have the children keep their worksheets in a folder or binder so that they can review the questions when they have quiet time to really sit and contemplate.
- Many of you have exercises in your repertoire that you've used successfully over the years that pertain to some of the topics. If it makes sense to you, combine my exercises with yours. You know your child or group best, so experiment to find a winning combination that works for all!

—⁓⋙⁓—

SET GROUND RULES FOR ALL LESSONS

- Participants should talk from the 'I' only, personal perspective—"I feel, I think, I view." This is the beginning of being responsible. Not everyone sees things the same way, feels the same, or has the same experience. There are major differences between people of the same race, religion, and gender. That is to say, everything in one's life is seen through the lens of personal experiences, beliefs, judgments and history.

- Children should talk about themselves, not about what mom, dad, siblings and friends did. You want them to bring personal experiences into the conversation.
- Children should not be allowed to cross talk, or try to fix or judge anyone.
- Create a safe space. Everything shared stays in the room. Children can share concepts with others, but not what someone else has shared personally.

SUGGESTED COURSE OF ACTION AS FACILITATOR

- Review the lesson beforehand. There are parent and facilitator notes at the beginning and end of each section to guide you.
- Think about the lesson and let it soak in.
- The lessons are meant to be read aloud as is, or paraphrased. As you become more comfortable presenting the program, it will be easier for you to put the lessons into your own words.
- Come up with references and/or experiences that your child or group can relate to directly.
- Ask questions and engage your kids. Get them to start thinking outside of the box.
- Be prepared to prod a little at first. Be patient and wait for kids to think of answers as they go within themselves.
- Remember they are not studying for a test. There is no one right answer. You are engaging in exploration into the soul.
- Encourage kids to dig deep. Go beyond surface answers and ordinary responses.
- If someone is being disruptive, move them to the back of the room or split up groups of friends. Don't let the children hide behind sarcasm to keep from going within.
- Trust that the program works. Trust the kids are receiving benefits even if you can't see them immediately. These are not quantifiable results. There's nothing to

test. However, pay attention to the feedback you receive and notice how the kids treat and interact with each other.

- I recommend you go through the entire workbook and do the exercises yourself. Dig deep. The more you open up to your divine self, the more impactful you can be. Kids feel energy. If you are resistant to change, the kids will be too. You are creating a vortex of energy for the kids to step into. Have you noticed when you're happy and generous those around you mirror (reflect back) your mood, they become happy and generous as well? But when you're in a bad mood, or angry, then you encounter people who mirror back that attitude to you?

- **Consciously create a loving and supportive space for learning and development. Bring your best self to the conversation!**

- Finally, remember if you make a difference with only one child, you have changed the world. Their light then shines on everyone they come into contact with. The results are exponential. Think about quality, not quantity. One child acting from compassion and integrity impacts a lot of people!

Lesson One

Grounding

❖ *PARENT AND FACILITATOR NOTES:*

> *I like to start off my programs with grounding. Grounding creates a strong foundation and helps foster an open and relaxed mind for receiving information. From here, I find it easier to build on the other lessons outlined in this workbook.*
>
> *Consciously create a loving and supportive space for learning, development and enlightenment by grounding yourself before you get started.*
>
> *After the opening question, pause and give children time to answer.*

—⁓〰⁓—

☯ *READ ENTIRE LESSON ALOUD AND/OR PARAPHRASE:*

Opening Questions: Have you ever heard of grounding yourself? What do you think it means?

GROUNDING DEFINITION AND WHY IT IS IMPORTANT:

A ship in the ocean drops its anchor to be grounded in one place. Otherwise, it would drift back out to sea. When you ground yourself, you bring your own energy back into your body and energy field. At times, your energy gets scattered.

You ground yourself to start thinking clearly and to receive divine guidance. You can't hear your intuition (inner voice) if you're scattered and frazzled. Grounding yourself gives you more access to communication with your higher self.

GROUNDING EXERCISE:

- Sit in a chair with your feet flat on the floor. (Children can sit on the floor, whatever is most comfortable for them.)
- Clear everything from your lap.
- Place hands on lap with palms either up or down.
- Close your eyes.
- Take 3 deep breaths. Relax your entire body.
- Picture in your mind's eye the area between your tail bone and pelvic region. (This is your first or root chakra. Chakra is an energy center. It is a Sanskrit word that means wheel.) You are going to ground this area to the center of the earth.
- Now you are going to create your grounding cord. Your grounding cord can be a big thick rope, or a tree trunk, or even a robust waterfall. Pick anything that feels solid and sturdy to you, something that will help you to feel anchored. Picture it in your mind's eye.
- Picture an anchor in the middle of your pelvic region.
- Wrap your grounding cord tightly around the anchor, then shoot it down to the center of the earth.
- Find a huge rock or tree to attach the end of your grounding cord to, then pull it tightly.
- You are now grounded. Allow yourself to relax into this experience. For some of you this may be the first time you've ever really felt grounded or anchored into your body.
- You can do this several times during the day to feel more peaceful and connected.

❖ *PARENT AND FACILITATOR NOTES:*

Copy and hand out the worksheet on the following page to review with the children after the exercise. Encourage the kids to share their experiences. Keep it light. Some children may not have been able to ground themselves the first time around. Remind them to have fun and not to worry if they didn't get it—just keep practicing. They will not be tested on their grounding technique or ability!

Have the kids put their worksheet in a folder or binder so that they can review the information at home.

☯ GROUNDING WORKSHEET

1. Were you able to visualize your first chakra and grounding cord? If not, don't worry, just keep practicing until you get it!

2. Do you feel different now that you are grounded?

3. Do you feel clearer mentally and emotionally?

Additional thoughts or questions:

(Remember to put this worksheet in your folder or binder to review later!)

Lesson Two

Affirmations

> *This lesson has a lot of explanatory information mixed in with the questions, but you can still engage kids in a two-way conversation. The explanations are essential for the children to grasp how important and powerful their thoughts are.*
>
> *Consciously create a loving and supportive space for learning, development and enlightenment by grounding yourself before you get started.*

—⚊—

☯ *READ ENTIRE LESSON ALOUD AND/OR PARAPHRASE:*

Opening questions: What is an affirmation? Can you give an example?

AFFIRMATION DEFINITION:

An affirmation is a declaration that something is true. It is a statement intended to provide encouragement, emotional support, or motivation.

But according to the Boulder Coaching Academy, "research has shown that we have between 45,000 and 51,000 thoughts a day. That's about 150 to 300 thoughts a minute. Research has also shown that for most people 80% of those thoughts are negative."

The study continues with, "Affirmations make you consciously aware of your thoughts. When you start making conscious positive thoughts, you actually become more aware of the negative thoughts that are always threatening to take over."

Do you think you use affirmations?
We all use affirmations whether consciously or subconsciously. There are things we affirm without even realizing it.

Can you name something you say over and over whether out loud or in your mind?

Why do some affirmations work and some don't you wonder?
Affirmations are always working, you just may not realize what you're telling yourself! If you go around saying things like "I'm stupid, it's too hard, nobody gets me" then that is exactly what will show up in your life.

Every word you speak is energy. This energy goes out of your mouth, into the air, into the world and is fulfilled. It is the same with your thoughts. Your thoughts are creating your life. It's time to pay attention to what you're thinking and saying! You have tremendous power rolled up inside of you. Use this power to your benefit, not to your detriment.

Let's use a pizza as an example: If you have a pizza cut into 10 slices and 8 of those slices are rotten (negative), then you can only eat 2 slices of pizza. What a waste of pizza! Well, you don't want to waste 8 out of 10 of your thoughts and words on negativity! Be careful about what you think and say because you are creating your life moment by moment.

AFFIRMATION EXERCISE:

- Come up with 2 positive affirmations that make you feel powerful and good.
- Keep them short and simple so they are easy to remember.
- Notice how you feel when you say them.

- Examples of affirmations:
  - I am worthy.
  - I am smart.
  - I have lots of good friends.
  - I enjoy learning.
  - Learning comes easily to me.
  - I always have everything I need.
  - I am healthy.
  - I am athletic.
  - I am helpful.

❖ *PARENT AND FACILITATOR NOTES:*

Copy and hand out the worksheet on the following page to review with the children after the exercise. Encourage the kids to share their experiences. Remind them they are in a safe space.

Have the kids keep all their worksheets together in a folder or binder so that they can review the information at home.

1. Scott Armstrong. Boulder Coaching Academy. *What is an Affirmation? They will change your life forever!* (January 5, 2009). http://www.bouldercoachingacademy.com/category/affirmations.

☯ AFFIRMATION WORKSHEET:

1. Did you identify any negative thoughts that you were unaware of?

2. Write down your two supportive affirmations.

3. How did it make you feel to say your positive affirmations to yourself?

4. Repeat your affirmations throughout the day several times.

Additional thoughts or questions:

(Remember to put this worksheet in your folder or binder to review later!)

Lesson Three

Intuition

❖ *PARENT AND FACILITATOR NOTES:*

This would be a good time to bring in a prop to help the kids make the connection between using life tools and physical tools (items) in their lives. I brought in my travel backpack filled with a flashlight, toilet paper, and wet naps, etc. The children laughed at the toilet paper, but I explained I've used it quite a bit while traveling internationally. The point of showing them my backpack was to compare it to the arsenal of tools they can develop to make their lives easier and more comfortable. The 21 lessons that they're learning with this program are providing them with tools to use in their life. Life tools are just as imperative as the physical tools they use.

Feel free to come up with your own analogy and props, or use my backpack example. I found that showing something physical and tangible helped to anchor in the relevance of these lessons in the children's lives.

Consciously create a loving and supportive space for learning, development and enlightenment by grounding yourself before you get started.

Reminder: after each question, pause and give children time to answer to create a two-way conversation with them.

―⁓⁓―

☯ *READ ENTIRE LESSON ALOUD AND/OR PARAPHRASE:*

Opening Questions: What is intuition? Can you see intuition?

INTUITION DEFINITION:

Intuition is your 6th sense—your sense of knowing. You may not know how you know something, you just do. You feel the awareness inside, it's not something you can see.

Why don't you recognize your intuition?

Most people rely on their five senses for information. They believe only what they can see, hear, taste, touch or smell, and often times ignore their intuition—their gut feeling. Intuition is a muscle that needs to be developed. You wouldn't go to the gym once and expect to look like a body builder, would you? The same is true with your intuition—the more you use and follow your internal guidance, the more confident and connected you will feel.

How can you tell the difference between your intuition and ego voice?

Your intuition is connected with your higher self and provides love, clarity, peace, compassion and guidance. It is expansive and inclusive. Your ego voice wants to protect the small, selfish you. When you're listening to your ego, things may feel like a struggle, usually somebody loses, you may have to justify your actions, you probably won't feel peaceful or loving, and you may feel limited, not expansive and inclusive.

Do you have any examples of using intuition in your life?

We all have and use intuition on a regular basis. For example: maybe you are at the mall and feel compelled to go into a store you would never go into, and you find that perfect toy or gadget you've been wanting. Or you have the thought to call your friend, and they answer by saying "I was just thinking about you." You have tapped into your internal voice and followed its guidance!

INTUITION EXERCISE:

You are going to practice stillness and connecting with your breath.

- Close your eyes and count to 20.
- Count on each 'in' breath and 'out' breath. (On 'one' breathe in. On 'two' breathe out. Keep counting and breathing until you reach 20.)
- Connect with your inner voice of knowing and wisdom.
- Silently ask a question.
- Listen for the answer. Notice any pictures or images, feelings or impressions.
- When you're ready, open your eyes and bring your attention back to the room.

Sometimes intuitive thoughts happen in a flash. Like you're walking out the door and you suddenly remember something you need for the day.

Start paying attention to and following these subtle instructions for your life.

—⁓—

❖ *PARENT AND FACILITATOR NOTES:*

Copy and hand out the worksheet on the following page to review with the children after the exercise. Encourage the kids to share their experiences. Make it light and have fun!

Have the kids keep all their worksheets together in a folder or binder so that they can review the information at home.

☯ INTUITION WORKSHEET:

1. Was your question answered during the quiet period?

2. Are you starting to remember hints of intuition in your life?

3. Are you willing to follow your internal guidance?

4. Practice listening to and following your intuition daily.

Additional thoughts or questions:

(Remember to put this worksheet in your folder or binder to review later!)

Lesson Four

Decision vs. Choice

❖ *PARENT AND FACILITATOR NOTES:*

> *Consciously create a loving and supportive space for learning, development and enlightenment by grounding yourself before you get started.*

> *Reminder: after each question, pause and give children time to answer. By this time, the children should be familiar and more comfortable with the format.*

---⟋⟍⟋---

☯ *READ ENTIRE LESSON ALOUD AND/OR PARAPHRASE:*

Opening Questions: What is a decision and what is a choice? Aren't they the same thing? Well, to most people they are. They're used interchangeably all the time.

DECISION AND CHOICE DEFINITIONS:

For the purpose of this discussion, decisions are choices that you make after thinking about something. You may contemplate for awhile, weigh the positive and negative aspects, and consider the results from previous decisions before you actually pick a course of action.

A choice is looking at two or more options, then choosing the one that resonates with your heart. It is a preference because it is a preference in the moment, not based on past experience of the thing chosen. That is to say, "I choose strawberries because I choose strawberries." No explanation or reasoning involved.

Why does this even matter?
Many decisions are made from fear, the past or other influences. Choices are simply made from affinities in the moment.

Beliefs, judgments, history and assumptions all weigh into decision-making. Often times, you do things out of habit and programming without even realizing it.

Choices open up new possibilities. You feel into your heart then you choose. Your choice may be completely unexpected to you and those around you, but you have stepped out of the known and predictable and into a dimension of opportunity and individuality.

Have you heard of *The Voice* television show?
The Voice is a singing competition with four coaches/judges. Contestants sing to the coaches who have their backs turned, hoping one will hear their voice and turn around. Prior to auditioning, the host always asks the contestant which coach they'll choose if given the opportunity. Some have been fantasizing for years about working with a particular coach. Then they get up there and chose someone completely different from who they thought they would choose. Why? Because they are totally in the moment of what feels right to them. They are connecting in the present and choosing from what's before them, rather than what they thought they wanted in the past.

Are choices better than decisions?
At times, it is certainly appropriate and advisable to contemplate and weigh your options before you make a decision. You don't want to be unnecessarily rash or reckless with your life. However, leave room for choice-making so that you can tap into the Universal Guidance that awaits ready to assist you. Remember, if you always do what you've always done, you'll keep getting the same results.

DECISION VS. CHOICE EXERCISE:

Think of a recent decision that you've made about something. How did you feel making it? Did you feel empowered, strong and courageous? Or did you feel stuck and burdened? Please explain.

Think about a time when you made a choice in the moment. How did you feel then?

———ᴍ———

❖ *PARENT AND FACILITATOR NOTES:*

Copy and hand out the worksheet on the following page to review with the children after the exercise. Encourage the kids to share their experiences.

Have the kids keep all their worksheets together in a folder or binder so that they can review the information at home.

☯ DECISION VS. CHOICE WORKSHEET:

1. Over the next few days, notice and/or log how many decisions you make as opposed to choices.

2. Pay attention to how you feel when you make decisions and choices.

3. Has anything new or unexpected occurred from a choice you made?

Additional thoughts or questions:

(Remember to put this worksheet in your folder or binder to review later!)

Lesson Five

Visualization

❖ *PARENT AND FACILITATOR NOTES:*

Consciously create a loving and supportive space for learning, development and enlightenment by grounding yourself before you get started.

Reminder: after each question, pause and give children time to answer. Encourage shy kids to engage in the conversation. Don't let them hide out. You want this to be an inclusive conversation.

—⟋⟍⟍⟋—

☯ *READ ENTIRE LESSON ALOUD AND/OR PARAPHRASE:*

Opening Questions: What is visualization? Do you think you've ever visualized anything?

VISUALIZATION DEFINITION:

To visualize means to see something in your mind's eye. To recall or form mental images or pictures.

What are the benefits of visualization?

- You get more of what you want with less effort.
- It increases your confidence. Practiced success leads to real success.
- Form always follows ideas: if you can see it you can be it.

- It increases focus (great mind training—you spend time thinking and creating what you want in a constructive manner which leaves less time for negative mind chatter).
- You have something to look forward to—your desired outcome.

Who uses visualization?

Everyone, all the time! Either negatively or positively.

- Negatively: Every time you worry about the future, are afraid something bad is going to happen, see yourself failing, etc. you are using the power of visualization.
- Positively: Seeing yourself acing a test, accomplishing a goal, or being happy.

Why does visualization work?
- Because your mind can't tell the difference between actual activities and mental pictures, it sees everything as real.

VISUALIZATION EXERCISE:

- Visualize something that you desire. Maybe you would like to receive a new tablet, go to an amusement park, score a goal, win a contest, or complete a challenging assignment.
- See it clearly.
- How do you feel achieving/receiving it?
- Who's around you?
- What are you wearing?
- Be as vivid and descriptive as possible.
- Hold the mental picture for a few moments.

—〰—

❖ *PARENT AND FACILITATOR NOTES:*

Copy and hand out the worksheet on the following page to review with the children after the exercise. Encourage the kids to share their experiences.

Have the kids keep all their worksheets together in a folder or binder so that they can review the information at home.

☯ VISUALIZATION WORKSHEET:

1. What were you able to visualize?

2. Did it feel real to you?

3. Did you notice any resistance (feelings of not wanting to do the exercise?)

4. Spend a few minutes each day visualizing something you desire.

Additional thoughts or questions:

(Remember to put this worksheet in your folder or binder to review later!)

Lesson Six

Mindfulness

❖ **PARENT AND FACILITATOR NOTES:**

This lesson has two different exercises to choose from. Plan ahead if you decide to do the second exercise as you will need a piece of food for each child.

Consciously create a loving and supportive space for learning, development and enlightenment by grounding yourself before you get started.

Reminder: after each question, pause and give children time to answer to create a two-way conversation with them.

—m—

☯ **READ ENTIRE LESSON ALOUD AND/OR PARAPHRASE:**

Opening Questions: What is mindfulness? Have you ever finished a meal and don't remember what the food tasted like because you were rushing or otherwise preoccupied? Do you think you were being mindful?

MINDFULNESS DEFINITION:

Mindfulness is being present to what you are doing. It is being in this moment with all of your thoughts and feelings without judgment of right or wrong, good or bad, and paying attention to what's around you.

What are ways that you are not mindful?
Examples could include:

- Driving or riding in a car
- Eating
- Watching television
- Sitting in class

How many times have you blanked out doing these activities?

What are ways that you are mindful during the day?
Possible discussion points:

- Doing homework
- Studying for a test
- Practicing an instrument or sport
- Playing with friends
- Playing video games
- Listening to music

Often times you are mindful without even knowing it. You're totally present in the moment, fully engaged with your activity and not worrying about what needs to be done later!

Why is it important to be mindful in your life?
When you are not mindful, you can miss things: information, experiences, a feeling of well-being. You can feel disconnected, ungrounded and separate. You may feel more like an observer of life rather than a participant.

MINDFULNESS EXERCISE: (SELECT ONE OF THE EXERCISES)

1. Choose a partner. For one minute look into their eyes fully and completely. What do you see? Notice everything. Share experiences with each other.

2. Put a piece of food in your mouth. How does it taste? What's the texture? Roll it around on your tongue. Think about where it came from. Who picked it? Where was it grown? How did it get here: was it grown locally or trucked or flown in? Pay attention to every detail.

—⟋⟍—

❖ *PARENT AND FACILITATOR NOTES:*

Copy and hand out the worksheet on the following page to review with the children after the exercise. Answer only the question that pertains to the exercise you just completed.

Have the kids keep all their worksheets together in a folder or binder so that they can review the information at home.

☯ MINDFULNESS WORKSHEET: (*ANSWER THE QUESTION THAT PERTAINS TO THE EXERCISE YOU COMPLETED.)

1a. *How did you feel being fully present with your partner? Comfortable or uncomfortable?

1b. *What did you notice about the food that you hadn't thought about before?

2. How do you think you can use mindfulness in your day to day life?

3. Practice being mindful the next time you eat. Notice the taste and texture of your food. Slow down and pay attention.

<u>Additional thoughts or questions:</u>

(Remember to put this worksheet in your folder or binder to review later!)

Lesson Seven

Gratefulness

❖ *PARENT AND FACILITATOR NOTES:*

This lesson has a lot of explanatory information so it may take a little longer. By the end, I want the children to feel empowered regardless of what's going on in their lives, and to recognize that just a small amount of gratitude can shift their vibration and outlook from dismal to hopeful.

Prepare a personal example of a challenge leading you in a different direction or creating something powerful in your life to share with the kids toward the end of the lesson. You'll see the Parent and Facilitator Notes icon.

Consciously create a loving and supportive space for learning, development and enlightenment by grounding yourself before you get started.

Reminder: after each question, pause and give children time to answer to create a two-way conversation with them.

—⁓—

☻ *READ ENTIRE LESSON ALOUD AND/OR PARAPHRASE:*
Opening Question: What is gratefulness?

GRATEFULNESS DEFINITION:

Gratefulness is feeling or showing thanks, appreciation or gratitude (usually for something or toward someone).

Can you think about gratefulness as a state of being?

True gratitude is not based upon conditions. If you wait for outer circumstances to change before you are grateful, then you'll always be waiting, wanting, hoping, or needing something or someone to be different before you can be happy.

Adopt an attitude of gratitude! The glass can either be half empty or half full depending on your perspective.

You can choose to look at life and situations positively or negatively. When you take a positive outlook you usually feel more powerful and hopeful, whereas a negative outlook can leave you feeling helpless and defeated.

What happens when you are grateful?

Gratefulness raises your vibration. The energy of being grateful goes out into the world and begins to attract more things in your life to be grateful for. New possibilities arise. Your mind opens up and you see things differently.

What if your situation is so bad or you see something so horrible you can't be grateful?

When you encounter a situation where you can't access gratefulness, then you can state this powerful affirmation over and over until you feel some sort of peace: "I bless this situation for the highest good of all concerned."

The minute you bless a situation, light begins to shine on it. This light brings love and healing for everyone involved. You cannot be a solution if you stay at the physical level of the problem. So, you shining light and bringing blessings raises the vibration of a circumstance so that healing can occur.

Bless a situation over and over until you feel the energy shift. You'll know when this happens because you will feel more peaceful and clear. Divine inspiration comes in and solutions that you never thought about or didn't know were possible present themselves. Trust that somehow whatever is going on is a step to other things. Hold onto that thought all day to empower yourself. You don't have to be dependent on others to find peace within yourself.

Often times when you look back on a circumstance that you didn't understand at the time, you have an 'aha' moment. You see how that situation propelled you to be better or do better. Amazing things have been created from people's greatest challenges!

—⁓⁓⁓—

❖ PARENT AND FACILITATOR NOTES:

This is a good place to give a personal example of a challenge you faced that turned out to be a blessing, or at least a positive step to other things.

—⁓⁓⁓—

GRATEFULNESS EXERCISE:

Think of three things that you are grateful for.

Examples:

- Hot water to take a shower
- Food to eat
- Being able to walk, talk and think
- Having heat to keep you warm and air conditioning to keep you cool
- Having friends

—⁓⁓⁓—

❖ *PARENT AND FACILITATOR NOTES:*

Copy and hand out the worksheet on the following page to review with the children after the exercise. Encourage the kids to share their experiences.

Have the kids keep all their worksheets together in a folder or binder so that they can review the information at home.

☯ GRATEFULNESS WORKSHEET:

1. Was it difficult to find three things to be grateful for?

2. How do you think adopting gratitude into your daily thoughts will impact your life?

3. Silently bless (instead of curse) things that disturb you and see what happens.

<u>Additional thoughts or questions:</u>

(Remember to put this worksheet in your folder or binder to review later!)

Lesson Eight

Meditation

❖ *PARENT AND FACILITATOR NOTES:*

Consciously create a loving and supportive space for learning, development and enlightenment by grounding yourself before you get started.

Reminder: after each question, pause and give children time to answer to create a two-way conversation with them.

———〰———

☯ *READ ENTIRE LESSON ALOUD AND/OR PARAPHRASE:*

Opening Question: What is meditation?

MEDITATION DEFINITION:

There are many different types of meditations, but in general, to meditate means to quiet your mind, to contemplate or reflect, or to actively practice mindfulness (concentrating on your breath or by repeating a word or statement) to reach higher levels of awareness.

Do any of you meditate?
If yes: What's your process? How long have you been meditating? Do you feel and act differently when you meditate and when you don't?

If no one meditates, move on to the Benefits of Meditation Section below.

What are the benefits of meditation?

Meditation helps you develop concentration, clear thinking, emotional positivity, calm seeing, peacefulness, joy and connectedness.

Establishing a regular meditation practice can help you feel more grounded and re-laxed. When you take time out each day to focus and quiet your mind, you are increasing your self-awareness and reducing your stress, thereby opening up access to hear your intuition (inner guidance.)

Why does meditation work?

Meditation calms your mind and body. It helps you focus your attention and helps you to see things more clearly. Visualizations and mindfulness exercises can be done during meditation.

GUIDED MEDITATION EXERCISE:

- Sit in a chair with your feet flat on the floor or sit on the floor.
- Close your eyes.
- Lay your hands with your palms down or up on your lap, or gently clasp hands together.
- Get comfortable (that's most important).
- Ground yourself using the grounding technique we discussed earlier.
- Take in three deep breaths. Relax your mind and body.
- Do not entertain any thoughts that may arise, simply let them pass.
- Keep your attention focused on relaxing and connecting with your higher self.
- Picture a golden sun hovering above your head. *(Pause)* Let this light cleanse and purify your body and energy field. *(Pause)* With each breath that you take draw in more of the sun's healing energy. Relax. *(Pause)* Let this brilliant light burn out any confusion, sadness, or discomfort you may be experiencing. Take in another deep breath. *(Pause)* Sit quietly for the next minute basking in the healing that is taking place.
- Now bring your attention and awareness back into the room. Slowly open your eyes when you're ready.

❖ *PARENT AND FACILITATOR NOTES:*

Copy and hand out the worksheet on the following page to review with the children after the exercise. Encourage the kids to share their experiences. Some children may not have been able to visualize the golden sun. Let them know it's okay—just keep practicing.

Have the kids keep all their worksheets together in a folder or binder so that they can review the information at home.

☯ MEDITATION WORKSHEET:

1. Were you able to visualize the sun over your head shining light into you? If not, just keep practicing. Have fun and play with it!

2. Establish a meditation routine. Meditating ten minutes a day is better than one hour a week. Meditate around the same time each day. Consistency is key!

3. Pay attention to how you feel when you meditate and when you don't.

Additional thoughts or questions:

(Remember to put this worksheet in your folder or binder to review later!)

Lesson Nine

Goals vs. Intentions

❖ *PARENT AND FACILITATOR NOTES:*

This lesson discusses goals and intentions. Keep in mind, the goals and intentions for a 6 year old will be different than those of a teenager. Gear your possible discussion points to suit your age range or use the ones provided.

Consciously create a loving and supportive space for learning, development and enlightenment by grounding yourself before you get started.

Reminder: after each question, pause and give children time to answer to create a two-way conversation with them.

—⁓—

☯ *READ ENTIRE LESSON ALOUD AND/OR PARAPHRASE:*

Opening Questions: What is an intention? Is it different than a goal?

GOALS AND INTENTION DEFINITION:

Goals and intentions are very similar. They are both something that you plan or intend to carry out, an aim or desired result.

What are some of your goals?
Possible discussion points:

- To make the school (basketball, volleyball, track) team.
- To graduate.
- To be a professional athlete.
- To be a veterinarian.
- To get my favorite toy for my birthday.
- To get a dog.

How do you plan to meet your goals?
Possible discussion points:

- Practice my favorite sport two hours each day.
- Study several hours weekly.
- Remind my parents regularly of the toy I want.
- Beg my parents for a dog.

What do you think the difference is between intentions and goals?
Goals are very specific and measurable. Your goal may be to run 10 laps, swim one mile, or lose five pounds in two weeks. Once you have your goal, then you set your tasks and specific actions to accomplish these goals: train every day, go on a diet, etc.

Setting goals is a linear process. It's based on what you know or think you know. If you don't know how to reach your goal, you may do research, then follow someone's advice on how to accomplish it.

On the other hand, intentions tap into your true self and the Universe. They can be similar to goals, but the process of fulfillment is different. You may intend on being a good student, having nice friends, or being a star athlete. When you set an intention, you then step back and wait for inspired actions rather than planned out actions. Intentions tap into miracles and the unknown because you are divinely guided in your movements. There is still work to be done and steps to take, but you're tuning into your intuition and following that higher guidance with inspired actions.

What is an inspired action?
Inspired actions come from your heart and intuition. They are internal impulses you receive once you've set an intention. Here's a real-life example to illustrate the author's point:

Sandra's family set the intention to move from Georgia to Florida for a winter. At the time, they didn't have the money to move, nor a place to stay, nor work for her husband. But they were clear that they wanted to be in Florida. Shortly after setting their intention, Sandra's husband was **inspired** to put an ad on Craig's List offering to exchange remodeling work for housing. His ad was answered by a couple who had a beautiful empty house in Florida that they wanted remodeled. Within a couple of weeks of setting their clear intention, they packed their cars and moved to Florida. Sandra's family now had a place to live in, and her contractor husband had work lined up! When they set their intention, they had no idea how it would work out.

This is the power of intentions; you tap into the unknown and true miracles become available!

INTENTION EXERCISE:
Come up with three intentions for the week. Pay attention to the unexpected.

—ᗰ—

❖ *PARENT AND FACILITATOR NOTES:*

Copy and hand out the worksheet on the following page to review with the children after the exercise. Two of the questions will need to be answered after several days to see if their intentions were fulfilled.

Have the kids keep all their worksheets together in a folder or binder so that they can review the information at home.

☯ INTENTION WORKSHEET:

1. What intentions did you set?

2. Were your intentions fulfilled?

3. What happened that you didn't know was possible?

Additional thoughts or questions:

(Remember to put this worksheet in your folder or binder to review later!)

Lesson Ten

Downtime

> *Consciously create a loving and supportive space for learning, development and enlightenment by grounding yourself before you get started.*
>
> *Reminder: after each question, pause and give children time to answer to create a two-way conversation with them.*

―∽∿∿∽―

☯ *READ ENTIRE LESSON ALOUD AND/OR PARAPHRASE:*

Opening question: What is downtime?

DOWNTIME DEFINITION:

When we think of downtime, we often think of a machine or computer being out of action or not available. Machines need downtime for maintenance and repairs, otherwise they would eventually burn out and be useless.

People need downtime as well! Otherwise we would eventually burn out and be useless just like machines.

Downtime is taking time out to do nothing (or doing very little).

Are you comfortable doing nothing?
Do you feel that resting is laziness? Do you call people who do take time to rest a "couch potato" or other negative term? In many Latin countries, siestas (afternoon naps) are common-place. Some businesses close, people take a break from work and school and rest.

In the United States, quite often we feel that the busier we are the more productive we are. Culturally we're a busy nation. Oftentimes people run themselves ragged before they will take a break.

Do you take regular downtime? Why or why not?
Possible discussion points:

- Do you feel that you never have enough time?
- Do you think that you don't need a break?
- Do you think resting is a waste of time?

Why is downtime important?

- Taking regular downtime allows you to rejuvenate before you get mentally and physically exhausted.
- Downtime allows you to connect with yourself and the Universe by creating a quiet space within yourself. You can hear your intuition better when you are quiet.
- Visualization, meditation, affirmations, and mindfulness all are more effective when you take time to just be.

DOWNTIME EXERCISE:
Do nothing for two minutes. You can have your eyes open or closed. Sit or lie down.

—⁓—

❖ *PARENT AND FACILITATOR NOTES:*

Copy and hand out the worksheet on the following page to review with the children after the exercise. Encourage the kids to share their experiences.

Have the kids keep all their worksheets together in a folder or binder so that they can review the information at home.

☯ DOWNTIME WORKSHEET:

1. How did you feel doing nothing for 2 minutes?

2. Each day take at least 10 minutes of downtime.

3. Notice and write down your thoughts and feelings about your downtime.

<u>Additional thoughts or questions:</u>

(Remember to put this worksheet in your folder or binder to review later!)

Friendship

❖ *PARENT AND FACILITATOR NOTES:*

Consciously create a loving and supportive space for learning, development and enlightenment by grounding yourself before you get started.

Reminder: after each question, pause and give children time to answer to create a two-way conversation with them. The goal here is to get them thinking about their friendships on a deeper level.

———〰———

☯ *READ ENTIRE LESSON ALOUD AND/OR PARAPHRASE:*

Opening question: What is friendship?

FRIENDSHIP DEFINITION:

Friendship is a relationship with someone that you like, have a bond with and trust. It's usually with someone outside of your family.

What do you look for in a friend?

Qualities to bring up:

- Kindness (soft heart, warm, gentle)
- Compassion (sympathetic, concern for others, understanding)

- Honesty (truthful)
- Integrity (good character and principles)
- Loyalty (faithfulness, strong support)

What makes a good friend?

Possible discussion points:

- Someone I can have fun with.
- Someone I trust.
- Someone who looks out for me.
- Someone who doesn't talk behind my back.
- Someone who wants the best for me.

Are you a good friend? Why or why not? (refer to above):

Why is it important to have like-minded friends in your life?

You want friends that lift you up, not put/bring you down. You want friends that are supportive, encouraging, and accepting. You want friends that have similar beliefs, interests and morals. They don't have to agree with you or even understand you all the time, but you want friends that help you to be the best person you can be.

For example, maybe you love school, and desire to get good grades. Would it be beneficial for you to hang around someone who just wants to goof off and encourages you not to study? I'd say they are not being a good friend to you because they are pulling you away from your desires, not encouraging you to be your best,

Does being a good friend mean you always say and do what you think the other person wants?

No! You want to be your best self and you want your friend to be their best self with you. Sometimes you may experience ups and downs in your relationship, but that's totally natural and normal. True friendship has many different dimensions and expressions.

FRIENDSHIP EXERCISE:

Think about two of your friends. What qualities do you like best about them? Is there anything you don't like?

—∿—

❖ *PARENT AND FACILITATOR NOTES:*

Copy and hand out the worksheet on the following page to review with the children after the exercise. Encourage the kids to share their experiences.

Have the kids keep all their worksheets together in a folder or binder so that they can review the information at home.

☯ FRIENDSHIP WORKSHEET:

1. If you have anything that you don't like about your friends, how can you turn it into something positive?

2. Do you feel safe being yourself with your friends? Comfortable?

3. Can you be honest with your friends?

<u>Additional thoughts or questions:</u>

(Remember to put this worksheet in your folder or binder to review later!)

Lesson Twelve

Beliefs

You may want to substitute out my beliefs for your own to make this section more personal.

Consciously create a loving and supportive space for learning, development and enlightenment by grounding yourself before you get started.

Reminder: after each question, pause and give children time to answer to create a two-way conversation with them.

—⟋⟍—

☯ *READ ENTIRE LESSON ALOUD AND/OR PARAPHRASE:*

Opening Question: What is a belief?

BELIEF DEFINITION:

A belief is something that you accept as true or think exists. It could be a statement, idea, principle or thing. It is trust, faith or confidence in someone or something.

What are some things that you believe (proven or unproven)? Here are some of the author's beliefs:

- She believes people are fundamentally good.
- She believes she has a divine purpose here on earth.
- She believes you have a purpose here on earth that only you can fulfill.

Do you believe life is hard? Money doesn't grow on trees? You'll never have friends or ace that test?

Why is it important to look at your beliefs?
What you believe creates your life, your experiences, everything! What you truly believe is being mirrored (reflected) back to you from the world. Your life is an accumulation of your beliefs.

Do your beliefs support the life you want to live?
"How would I know?" you may wonder. Look around you. Are you happy and fulfilled? Peaceful and joy-filled? Or stressed and unhappy? Friendless and lonely?

Remember, the quality and content of your life is reflected back to you through your life experiences. Often times you are unconscious (not aware of thoughts that affect your actions and behaviors) about your beliefs. Once you identify and take responsibility for what you truly believe, you take responsibility for your life!! Some beliefs are easy to change—maybe you think you don't like Brussels sprouts, then you taste them again and love them! Some beliefs are hidden and difficult to uncover.

BELIEFS EXERCISE:
Identify a belief that doesn't support you. Be scientific, examine it, and go beyond surface answers and ordinary responses. If you feel stuck, look into your life and find something that causes you stress or discomfort to begin uncovering the unsupportive belief.

—⚋—

❖ *PARENT AND FACILITATOR NOTES:*

Copy and hand out the worksheet on the following page to review with the children after the exercise. Encourage the kids to share their experiences.

Have the kids keep all their worksheets together in a folder or binder so that they can review the information at home.

☯ BELIEFS WORKSHEET:

1. What belief were you able to uncover that doesn't support you?

2. Were you surprised by what came up?

3. Set an intention to release the unsupportive belief and to foster beliefs that support your peace and joy!

Additional thoughts or questions:

(Remember to put this worksheet in your folder or binder to review later!)

Lesson Thirteen

Blame vs. Responsibility

❖ *PARENT AND FACILITATOR NOTES:*

> *Some kids may be uncomfortable hearing they are responsible for their lives, so take your time with them and be extra gentle.*
>
> *Consciously create a loving and supportive space for learning, development and enlightenment by grounding yourself before you get started.*
>
> *Reminder: after each question, pause and give children time to answer to create a two-way conversation with them.*

—⁓—

☯ *READ ENTIRE LESSON ALOUD AND/OR PARAPHRASE:*

Opening Questions: What is blame? What is responsibility?

BLAME AND RESPONSIBILITY DEFINITIONS:

Blame means to accuse or find fault with someone or something; to point the finger at someone or something else (away from yourself) and place responsibility for an error or wrongdoing.

Responsibility means to be accountable for something; to act on your own, make decisions, or to stand up for something or someone in a positive way.

Which is a more powerful position and why?
Responsibility! The energy of blame is a lower vibration. Blaming can leave you feeling powerless. You have no control when you blame. You lose the ability to change a situation if you point the finger at someone or something else.

The energy of being responsible is a higher vibration. You have control and power. It's the energy of true leadership—the real movers and shakers.

Would you rather be around someone who blames or someone who is responsible? Who do you feel you can trust more? Why?
Example: Imagine you are on a team and your coach blames the players for the losing season. How would that make you feel? How about a coach that takes responsibility for the team's losses and vows to make corrections for next season. Which coach do you feel is an effective leader and which team would you rather be on?

The game of life is not about being perfect or not making mistakes. It's about making corrections when you find you are off track. It is only when you are accountable for your own actions that you have the power to make adjustments and create a different outcome. You can't affect positive change from the position of blame.

BLAME VS. RESPONSIBILITY EXERCISE:
Think about a time you were responsible, then think about a time you blamed someone else. Make each recollection as vivid as possible.

—ɯ—

❖ *PARENT AND FACILITATOR NOTES:*

Copy and hand out the worksheet on the following page to review with the children after the exercise. Encourage the kids to share their experiences.

Have the kids keep all their worksheets together in a folder or binder so that they can review the information at home.

☯ BLAME VERSUS RESPONSIBILITY WORKSHEET:

1. How did you feel when you were being responsible?

2. How did you feel when you were blaming?

3. Practice being responsible in your life.

Additional thoughts or questions:

(Remember to put this worksheet in your folder or binder to review later!)

Lesson Fourteen

Time Management

❖ *PARENT AND FACILITATOR NOTES:*

Consciously create a loving and supportive space for learning, development and enlightenment by grounding yourself before you get started.

Reminder: after each question, pause and give children time to answer to create a two-way conversation with them.

—∿—

☯ *READ ENTIRE LESSON ALOUD AND/OR PARAPHRASE:*

Opening Question: What is time management?

TIME MANAGEMENT DEFINITION:

Time management, in its simplest form, is the way you organize and plan how long you spend on specific activities. Activities can include: doing homework, practicing an instrument or sport, creating art, playing with friends, watching television or playing video games.

Why is this important at your age?

The sooner you learn how to organize and maximize your time, the less stress you will create for yourself. You'll get more accomplished with less effort and be more productive in your life.

Are you happy with how you manage your time? Why or why not?
Possible discussion points:

- Do you feel rushed doing homework?
- Do you spend enough time playing and hanging out with friends?
- Do you have enough quality family time?
- Do you take downtime?
- Do you have time for your projects?

What happens when you don't manage your time effectively?
You can miss deadlines and opportunities, your work quality suffers and you put undue pressure on yourself for running out of time to complete a project or task.

Let's look at time as energy, more holistically, instead of as a fixed thing:
You can expand and contract time, use it as something you can control instead of something that's limited. How? By settings intentions. Review what you want to get done, set the intention to get it done easily, effortlessly and on time, and allow your inspired actions and intuition to guide you.

Here's an example of how you may already do this without knowing it. Have you ever been running late for something and you say to yourself or to the Universe, "I plan on getting there in time." While in route, you seem to catch every green light, traffic is lighter than usual, and you make it to your destination in record time. Better yet, the start time was delayed or other people arrive at the same time you do or even later, so you end up missing nothing. You have bent time to support your intention.

Easy time management tips:

1. Write stuff down: playdates, school programs/projects, extracurricular commitments, homework and ideas. Once you write activities down, you don't have to waste your brain power trying to remember the things you need to do.

2. Do the most important things first. For example, if you have an assignment due in two days and one due in a week, work on the assignment due in two days first so that you don't run out of time, cut corners on the quality of your work, or miss the deadline altogether.

Do you have any time management tips to share?

TIME MANAGEMENT EXERCISE:

Think of one thing you usually do at the last minute that could be done earlier to reduce your stress.

—⁓〰⁓—

❖ *PARENT AND FACILITATOR NOTES:*

> *Copy and hand out the worksheet on the following page to review with the children after the exercise. Encourage the kids to share their experiences.*

> *Have the kids keep all their worksheets together in a folder or binder so that they can review the information at home.*

☯ TIME MANAGEMENT WORKSHEET:

1. Pay attention to how you view and use time. Is it expansive or constrictive?

2. Get a datebook or journal to keep track of your activities.

3. What habit would you like to change, and how could you go about changing it?

<u>Additional thoughts or questions:</u>

(Remember to put this worksheet in your folder or binder to review later!)

Lesson Fifteen

Boredom

❖ *PARENT AND FACILITATOR NOTES:*

Consciously create a loving and supportive space for learning, development and enlightenment by grounding yourself before you get started.

Reminder: after each question, pause and give children time to answer to create a two-way conversation with them.

—◆—

☯ *READ ENTIRE LESSON ALOUD AND/OR PARAPHRASE:*

Opening Question: What is boredom?

BOREDOM DEFINITION:

Boredom is not being interested in or happy with what's going on around you. It is feeling like you'd rather be doing something else (anything else!) more interesting or exciting. Boredom is feeling that your day is dull or tedious. You may find yourself sighing or yawning a lot when you are bored.

Why do you get bored?

The author's daughter says she's bored because she has nothing to do, but it's really that she wants attention.

Do you say you're bored when you really mean something else?
What is it that you really want to say?

Let's consider boredom as a creative space. What can you do about boredom?
Find something interesting to do. You can use boredom to propel you to try a new activity, or to create or invent something. If you're in a place you don't want to be, like an event with your parent and you can't leave, go within and practice mindfulness, visualization or meditation. Choose to use the time to your benefit.

Whose responsibility is it if you're bored?
Yours! Boredom is a choice. You can look at your circumstances as boring or find a golden nugget to focus on. You can use boredom to either cut off or encourage your creativity.

What do you do when you're bored that's not healthy for you?
Examples could include:

- Overeat
- Play video games for hours
- Watch television
- Sleep too much

BOREDOM EXERCISE:
How does boredom cut off your creativity?

How does boredom encourage your creativity?

—⟿—

❖ *PARENT AND FACILITATOR NOTES:*

Copy and hand out the worksheet on the following page to review with the children after the exercise. Encourage the kids to share their experiences.

Have the kids keep all their worksheets together in a folder or binder so that they can review the information at home.

☯ BOREDOM WORKSHEET:

1. Share a way that boredom cuts off your creativity.

2. Share an example of boredom encouraging your creativity.

3. The next time you say you're bored, think about if you really mean something else.

Additional thoughts or questions:

(Remember to put this worksheet in your folder or binder to review later!)

Lesson Sixteen

Anger, Part 1

❖ *PARENT AND FACILITATOR NOTES:*

This lesson may bring up some unexpected emotions. Be extra gentle and loving and take your time with it. You want your children to really think about the answers and have time to go within.

You may combine Anger, Part 1 and Anger, Part 2 if time permits.

Consciously create a loving and supportive space for learning, development and enlightenment by grounding yourself before you get started.

Reminder: after each question, pause and give children time to answer to create a two-way conversation with them.

—⚉—

☯ *READ ENTIRE LESSON ALOUD AND/OR PARAPHRASE:*

Opening Question: What is anger?

ANGER DEFINITION:

Anger is a strong feeling of displeasure, dislike or resentment. It can make you want to scream and pull your hair out or even hurt someone. It also gives you a way to express negative feelings, and can motivate you to find solutions to problems.

What are the different forms (or names) for anger?

- Frustration-feeling upset because you can't do or change something
- Irritation-feeling annoyed or impatient
- Annoyance-feeling inconvenienced
- Rage-violent, uncontrollable anger
- Upset-unhappy, disappointed, bothered

What makes you angry?
Possible Discussion Points:

- Does a brother or sister bother you?
- Do your parents keep you from doing something you want or make you do something you don't want to do?
- Does a teacher or friend upset you?
- Injustice?

How do you behave when you're angry?
Possible answers:

- Out of control (yell uncontrollably, throw or hit things, hurt yourself or others)
- Mean-spirited (wanting to punish or cause harm)
- Passive-aggressive (you act nice or like you're not upset, then you say or do things to hurt the person you're mad at)
- Sarcastic (biting humor)
- Short (impatient, cutting off someone)
- Dismissive (lack of interest, rejection)
- Cold (no affection)
- Shut down (quiet, hold your anger inside)
- Balanced (able to express your anger effectively and move on)

Is it okay to get angry? Do you feel okay being angry?

Anger can express emotions that you've been holding in and help you to get clarity by finally letting go of the bottled up emotions, but you don't want to stay in anger long. Prolonged anger lowers your vibration and can lead to sickness. And being angry just doesn't feel good. You are not joy-filled and peaceful when you're angry.

How do you feel when people get angry?

Are you scared? Uncomfortable? Cower in a corner or fight back? Or are you grounded and strong? Ideally you want to be grounded and strong so that you can stay in your power. You want to be clear and effective even when someone else is angry.

Is it better to be honest or a "people pleaser" for fear people will get mad at you?

Honest!! When you don't express yourself honestly, you usually end up being angry at yourself. Then blame can creep in and you can feel like a victim to the world around you. Also, being honest can shift a situation positively in ways that you may not have foreseen.

How/when do you get mad at yourself?

Possible discussion points:

- Failing an exam
- Losing a game
- Gaining or losing too much weight
- Not feeling handsome or pretty enough
- Making a mistake

ANGER, PART 1 EXERCISE:

Think of a time when you got angry. How did you behave or what did you do? What could you have done differently?

—⁓—

❖ PARENT AND FACILITATOR NOTES:

Copy and hand out the worksheet on the following page to review with the children after the exercise. Encourage the kids to share their experiences.

Have the kids keep all their worksheets together in a folder or binder so that they can review the information at home.

☯ ANGER, PART 1 WORKSHEET:

1. Would you feel differently about your life if you expressed yourself honestly and didn't hold things in?

2. How can you alleviate things in your life that make you angry?

3. Is there a different emotion rather than anger that you could choose to express yourself?

Additional thoughts or questions:

(Remember to put this worksheet in your folder or binder to review later!)

Lesson Seventeen

Anger, Part 2

❖ *PARENT AND FACILITATOR NOTES:*

Anger is such a vast topic that I broke it into two lessons. This lesson gives processes to release anger and should be less intense than Anger Part 1.

Consciously create a loving and supportive space for learning, development and enlightenment by grounding yourself before you get started.

Reminder: after each question, pause and give children time to answer to create a two-way conversation with them.

———〜〜〜———

☯ *READ ENTIRE LESSON ALOUD AND/OR PARAPHRASE:*

Opening Statement: Let's do a quick review from Anger, Part 1.

ANGER DEFINITION:

Anger is a strong feeling of displeasure, dislike or resentment. It also gives you a way to express negative feelings, and can motivate you to find solutions to problems.

Different forms (or names) for anger:

- Frustration-feeling upset because you can't do or change something
- Irritation-feeling annoyed or impatient
- Annoyance-feeling inconvenienced
- Rage-violent, uncontrollable anger
- Upset-unhappy, disappointed, bothered

Ways to release anger:

You don't want to hold onto anger for long because it doesn't feel good. You can't be creative or peaceful when you're angry. So express yourself, then release the anger from your body by trying any or all of the following techniques.

- Drink water (at least 8 ounces), helps soothe you, and calms your energy immediately.
- Close your eyes and breathe. Take deep relaxing breaths which will help release toxins created by anger.
- Find a place to be alone. Meditate, practice grounding and mindfulness.
- Go for a walk (inside or outside). Walking helps move energy.
- Go outside and get fresh air. Get into nature.
- Dance around your room unabashedly.
- Exercise--any type.
- Listen to music.
- Yell into your pillow.
- Sing in the shower.
- Relax/sleep.
- Drum on your body. Find a beat and rhythm that brings you joy.

Positive change can come from anger:

Anger has been the catalyst for social change throughout history. Here are just a few examples in the United States:

- MADD (Mothers Against Drunk Driving): was founded in 1980 by a mother who lost her 13-year-old daughter to a drunk driver. Its purpose is to end drunk, drugged and underage driving, and to support the victims of these crimes.
- Civil Rights Movement of the 1950's and 1960's: numerous nonviolent protests and civil disobedience acts such as boycotts and sit-ins took place to end racial segregation. The results included: schools were desegregated, interracial marriages were legalized, passage of the 23rd Amendment (District of Columbia gained the right to vote in presidential elections), the 24th Amendment (prohibits payment of taxes to vote), and the Voting Rights Act of 1965 (prohibits racial discrimination in voting), among many others.
- Women's Voting Movement in the 1920's: resulted in the 19th Amendment, which gave women the right to vote.

ANGER, PART 2 EXERCISE:

Think of a time when you used your anger for positive change.

———〜〜〜———

❖ *PARENT AND FACILITATOR NOTES:*

Copy and hand out the worksheet on the following page to review with the children after the exercise. Encourage the kids to share their experiences.

Have the kids keep all their worksheets together in a folder or binder so that they can review the information at home.

☯ ANGER, PART 2 WORKSHEET:

1. The next time you get angry, use one of the techniques described to release the anger.

2. Come up with positive ways of your own to release anger.

3. Practice channeling your anger into positive outcomes. Set intentions to do so and let your intuition guide you.

<u>Additional thoughts or questions:</u>

(Remember to put this worksheet in your folder or binder to review later!)

Lesson Eighteen

Complaining

❖ *PARENT AND FACILITATOR NOTES:*

You may want to substitute a personal example of a time you complained and it resulted in getting something you wanted. (Under 'Is Complaining Useful' question.)

Consciously create a loving and supportive space for learning, development and enlightenment by grounding yourself before you get started.

Reminder: after each question, pause and give children time to answer to create a two-way conversation with them.

———ɯɯ———

☯ *READ ENTIRE LESSON ALOUD AND/OR PARAPHRASE:*

Opening Question: What is complaining?

COMPLAINING DEFINITION:

To complain means to express dissatisfaction with something or someone. It is when you are constantly finding fault.

What do you complain about?

Complaining can be done either verbally (out loud to others) or non-verbally (in your head).

Possible discussion points:

Do you complain about a teacher?

Do you complain about your weight?

Do you complain about the weather, it's either too hot or too cold?

Do you complain about your parent's cooking?

Is complaining useful?

Sometimes. It can create change (like anger and social movements), or complaining can help you get what you want. For example, the author complained to the General Manager at her gym because they didn't have proper adult supervision in the kids' club and some kids were being aggressive and inconsiderate, so they brought in another adult to help out.

When is complaining not useful?

When it's pointless. For example, complaining that you're thirsty instead of getting a glass of water. Or you've already taken care of a situation but you're still griping about it. Or maybe you are venting to somebody about someone else instead of dealing with the person directly.

What's the problem with too much complaining?

It lowers your vibration, people won't want to be around you, and it's difficult to be creative and a contribution when you're always complaining.

COMPLAINING EXERCISE:

Think of something you complain about and come up with a specific action to resolve the complaint.

—⌇⌇—

❖ *PARENT AND FACILITATOR NOTES:*

Copy and hand out the worksheet on the following page to review with the children after the exercise. Encourage the kids to share their experiences.

Have the kids keep all their worksheets together in a folder or binder so that they can review the information at home.

☯ COMPLAINING WORKSHEET:

1. Do you complain more about yourself or others?

2. When you catch yourself complaining (either verbally or in your head), stop and notice. Intend to choose more powerful thoughts?

3. Notice how you feel around someone who complains a lot. Do you want to be around them?

<u>Additional thoughts or questions:</u>

(Remember to put this worksheet in your folder or binder to review later!)

Lesson Nineteen

Stress

> *Consciously create a loving and supportive space for learning, development and enlightenment by grounding yourself before you get started.*
>
> *Reminder: after each question, pause and give children time to answer to create a two-way conversation with them.*

—〰—

☯ *READ ENTIRE LESSON ALOUD AND/OR PARAPHRASE:*

Opening Question: What is stress?

STRESS DEFINITION:

Stress is frustration, worry, feeling pressure about something, or feeling overwhelmed. It is mental or emotional strain and discomfort. It's your body's way of responding to any kind of demand.

What happens when you're stressed?

You may sweat, get nervous, feel tense, start rushing, become impatient, become hyper-focused, get a stomach ache or headache, get thirsty, feel overall malaise, or have eating or sleeping problems.

Why do you get stressed?
Possible discussion points:

- You have too little time to get things done.
- You're worrying about something.
- You have too many things to do.
- You don't want to do something or don't know how.

Do you think there is good stress and bad stress?
Sometimes stress can be a motivator, like when giving a speech, doing a new sport, or getting out of trouble (adrenals kick in).

But ongoing stress wears on your body: being bullied or teased consistently, dealing with a stressful situation at home, being behind in or not understanding your schoolwork, having too many activities, or not having enough food are chronic causes of strain that can affect your health and well-being.

Ways to minimize stress:

- Don't overschedule.
- Don't try to be perfect.
- Get a good night's sleep.
- Learn to relax (take deep breaths, walk, drink water, get out in nature).
- Exercise regularly.
- Watch your thoughts (is the bottle half empty or full?).
- Solve little problems as soon as possible.
- Ask for help, tell an adult if you have a problem!

STRESS EXERCISE:
Think of a way you can minimize a stressful situation in your life.

—⟳—

❖ *PARENT AND FACILITATOR NOTES:*

Copy and hand out the worksheet on the following page to review with the children after the exercise. Encourage the kids to share their experiences.

Have the kids keep all their worksheets together in a folder or binder so that they can review the information at home.

☯ STRESS WORKSHEET:

1. Practice dealing with small problems as they arise instead of avoiding them.

2. Ask a parent or teacher for help with a situation you would normally try to deal with on your own.

3. Get more sleep and notice how you feel.

<u>Additional thoughts or questions:</u>

(Remember to put this worksheet in your folder or binder to review later!)

Lesson Twenty

Happiness

❖ *PARENT AND FACILITATOR NOTES:*

I played the song "Happy" by Pharrell Williams to get the kids moving. Some loved the song and danced, while others disliked it and stood still waiting impatiently for it to end. Use your discretion before trying this with your group.

Consciously create a loving and supportive space for learning, development and enlightenment by grounding yourself before you get started.

Reminder: after each question, pause and give children time to answer to create a two-way conversation with them.

—⟋⟍⟍⟋—

☯ *READ ENTIRE LESSON ALOUD AND/OR PARAPHRASE:*

Opening Question: What is happiness?

HAPPINESS DEFINITION:

Happiness is being joyful, delighted, in good spirits, satisfied, light-hearted, and fulfilled.

Does having a happy life mean you always feel good and don't have any problems?
No! Life is made up of all the ups and downs we experience. Facing sadness or disappointment makes the joy more meaningful. Your attitude also determines your happiness level. Do you see a glass as half empty or half full? (The 2015 movie *Inside Out* is a great example of how our emotions are interconnected and create a whole, full life-experience.)

What makes you happy?
Possible discussion points:

- Having friends
- Volunteering or helping people
- Being with your family
- Doing well in school
- Playing sports or participating in activities

Do you have to work at being happy?
Yes and no. For some people, being happy is constant work. It takes discipline, mindfulness, gratitude, and positive attitude to be happy. For others, happiness is more organic and natural.

Who's responsible for your happiness?
You are!! How you experience and deal with life and your problems depends on you.

Are rich people happier than poor people?
Not necessarily.

Does a higher education make you happier?
Not necessarily.

True, lasting happiness won't be found in the material world. Happiness is found within yourself, in your heart. Making choices that support you, being grateful and mindful, feeling connected to a higher power, controlling your mind chatter, and setting powerful intentions will aid you in being happy.

HAPPINESS EXERCISE:

Remember a time when you were happy. Feel the emotions throughout your entire body. Let yourself smile or laugh. Fully embody this experience.

❖ *PARENT AND FACILITATOR NOTES:*

Copy and hand out the worksheet on the following page to review with the children after the exercise. Encourage the kids to share their experiences.

Have the kids keep all their worksheets together in a folder or binder so that they can review the information at home.

☯ HAPPINESS WORKSHEET:

1. Pick something to do each day that brings you joy.

2. Laugh several times a day, even if you don't feel like it. (Laughter immediately raises your vibration and makes you feel good.)

3. Use positive affirmations to proclaim your happiness (I am happy, I am joy-filled, I am peaceful).

Additional thoughts or questions:

(Remember to put this worksheet in your folder or binder to review later!)

Lesson Twenty-One

Compassion

❖ *PARENT AND FACILITATOR NOTES:*

Consciously create a loving and supportive space for learning, development and enlightenment by grounding yourself before you get started.

Reminder: after each question, pause and give children time to answer to create a two-way conversation with them.

———ɱ———

☻ *READ ENTIRE LESSON ALOUD AND/OR PARAPHRASE:*

Opening Question: What is compassion?

COMPASSION DEFINITION:

Compassion is showing sympathy, pity, empathy, care, concern, kindness, sensitivity, and love.

Let's talk about compassion as a way of being, as an intention for your life:
According to Lee Carroll, an international author and speaker, "the energy of compassion is not an emotion, it is a state of mind. It combines empathy, love and introspection."

In other words, compassion is not an emotion that you feel toward someone or a situation, then it goes away. Compassion is not fleeting when you have it as an intention for who you want to be in the world.

Why is compassion important? Especially for yourself?
The energy and vibration of compassion are high. When others are reacting with fear and anger, you being compassionate and balanced lifts the vibration of those around you. What you do and how you're being shifts your environment. Can you listen without having to argue or defend your point of view? Are you understanding? Do people want to be with you? Are you helping humanity or are you part of the problem?

It's important to be compassionate with yourself as well. Love and honor who you are. Be gentle and caring. Don't beat yourself up when you're not perfect. Being compassionate with yourself helps you to be more compassionate with others.

How do you feel when people aren't compassionate?
Possible discussion points:

- Bad and wrong
- Small
- Angry
- Misunderstood
- Isolated

Bottom line, not good.

COMPASSION EXERCISE:
Think of a way to be more compassionate to others and to yourself.

—◊—

❖ *PARENT AND FACILITATOR NOTES:*

Copy and hand out the worksheet on the following page to review with the children after the exercise. Encourage the kids to share their experiences.

Have the kids keep all their worksheets together in a folder or binder so that they can review the information at home.

1. Lee Carroll. *Kryon - Compassion is the Highest form of Energy for Human* (March 15, 2016)
   https://www.youtube.com/watch?v=ytaI48O7e1g

☯ COMPASSION WORKSHEET:

1. How would being compassionate with yourself shift how you feel about your life?

2. How would being compassionate toward others shift how you act in the world?

3. How would being compassionate toward others shift how you the view world?

Additional thoughts or questions:

(Remember to put this worksheet in your folder or binder to review later!)

Wrap Up!

Congratulations, you have completed the program of 21 Lessons To Empower The New Age Kid! Although you've reached the end of the workbook, it's really just the beginning of your child's or group's journey to transformation. Each time you review the lessons, you have the opportunity to reveal hidden beliefs and judgments that keep children from living outrageously magnificent lives. Think of the journey as peeling off layers of an onion—there are several sections to uncover until your reach the core.

Keep reviewing and practicing the lessons. So much is available for you and the children that you can't even begin to imagine. You now have a common language and tools to use for learning and development. If you're group is restless or unruly, you can tell them to ground themselves and they'll all know exactly what you mean. Better yet, you may find the kids reminding each other to use the lessons when a problem or situation arises—they're taking responsibility for their environment! My daughter enjoys encouraging me to use the principles she's learned, consequently, we get to hold each other accountable for who we're being in the world.

―∿―

WHERE DO YOU GO FROM HERE?

You can create Open Forum Discussions! I did this at the end of the presentations with my daughter's homeschool group and was thrilled by the depth of the conversation. The concept is, ask the kids what they want to talk about, then have them vote on the topics suggested. Give children parameters—the topics need to be life principles and lessons, not some random question like, "Why do fish swim in schools in the ocean?"

Once the topic is agreed upon, ask the kids what they want to discuss about it. Let them generate the questions and discussion under your guidance. Follow the same structure as the lessons in the workbook and request that they come up with the exercise as well.

A few cool things occurred during an Open Forum Discussion about awkwardness that we had: kids that hadn't fully participated eagerly raised their hands with suggestions, topics I hadn't thought about were brought up, and the kids were very passionate, sincere and open in talking about feeling awkward in their lives.

By this time, a flow and format have been established to create spontaneous, powerful discussions. Countless topics can be covered as you can imagine!

Most importantly, enjoy the process of it all. The road to self-discovery and enlightenment is a never-ending journey, so you might as well have fun along the way!

Resource List

For those of you who still want more, here's a list of resources to dig deeper into some of the concepts covered in this book—they are totally optional, of course!

Doreen Virtue, *Indigo, Crystal and Rainbow Children*.
http://www.angeltherapy.com/blog/indigo-crystal-and-rainbow-children

Lee Carroll and Jan Tober, *The Indigo Children: The New Kids Have Arrived*. Paperback – May 1, 1999.

Nikki Pattillo, *Star Children*.
http://www.starchildren.info/crystal.html.

Carolyne Fuqua, Ph.D., *Impartial Self-Observation: The Key to Self-Realization*. Paperback – 2003.

Michael Bernard Beckwith, *Spiritual Liberation: Fulfilling Your Soul's Potential*. Paperback – October 6, 2009

Dr. Hew Len, *Ho'oponopono (Forgiveness)*
https://youtu.be/z97pS-f0WMY

My original sketch that Thomas used to create my beautiful cover art!

NOTES:

NOTES:

NOTES:

NOTES:

NOTES:

NOTES:

94124237R00067

Made in the USA
Columbia, SC
19 April 2018